Zora's Letters

Iryna Colvin-Spencer

Zora's Letters

Print Paperback ISBN: 979-8-9850290-8-6
eBook ISBN: 979-8-9850290-3-1

Published, and distributed by:
ICSpencer Publications
29 Hawthorne Trl
Depew, New York 14043
Tel: (716) 289-7610
Email: icspencerwriter@gmail.com

Interior and cover design by: TeaBerryCreative.com

PERSONAL DEDICATION

*To my entire loving family, Chutko,
Piusienski, Colvin, Spencer, Teluk, who have
encouraged me to pursue my dream.*

*To all those who believe as I do, that the animals
we adopt are an integral part of our family, and
deserve loving care, protection and a safe home.
If you want to judge a person's character observe
how they interact with your children and pets.*

ZORA'S DEDICATION

I'm dedicating this book to my entire family.
How fortunate I am to have all of them in my life.
They all hold a special place in my heart.
They say I have unconditional love,
but they serve as a constant reminder of
what unconditional love is all about.

High Five! Wuff you!
Zora

Please Donate to Animal Shelters everywhere.

ACKNOWLEDGMENTS

A heartfelt thank you to my daughter, Julianne (Piusienski) Renczkowski, a/k/a Sissy, the voice of Zora, whose support and encouragement were instrumental in publishing this book. A special thank you to my husband Lee Spencer and all the Spencer family members, my son Thaddeus (Ted) Piusienski, Jr., his two children, my granddaughter Lauren and grandson Colin, my sister, and best friend Maria and her husband Paul Teluk, their four children and grandchildren. My brother Robert aka Bob (Mike) Sowards, 'who made it through that fateful night' and his son, Larry. A special thank you to Julianne's two daughters, my granddaughters Natasha and Michala, and my son-in-law Bill, who provided Zora with a second home. My adopted families, Holobickyj and Chomyn.

I would like to acknowledge the Colvin clan, and my support network and closest friends My LIB Ladies, Maria, Nicky, Betty, Delphine, Mary, Halyna, and Irka; my special friends,

Susan Baumler-Spitzer, Jeanne Conklin, Lori Caradori, and Eileen Lambert for their continued support.

A special thank you to Becky Bermingham, of "The Grooming Post", who has kept Zora groomed to the nines.

Thank you all from the bottom of my heart.

Contents

Zora's Family Tree

MOMMY	DADDY—LEE

Sissy (Julianne), Uncle Bill, Natasha,
Michala, Roxy, Jingles and Nala

Uncle Ted, Lauren, Colin, Max

Aunt Mary and Uncle Paul

Uncle Mike (Robert—Bob),
Larry, Justin and Wesley (Wes)

IT'S ALL ABOUT ME—YES, IT IS

I was one of three fur babies in my parent's home in Ohio. That family decided they didn't want me so they sold me to a lady in Western New York telling everyone I was going to be a show dog.

My foster mother picked me up when I was only nine weeks old, and then two months later decided I was not as pretty as she first thought. She told me I was not perfect. I did not meet Shih Tzu show dog standards. She stated she hoped she could sell me to someone for the money she paid for me. Well, that did a lot for my self-esteem? I still maintained my outgoing personality, because I really didn't understand what was happening.

Then one day this lady, her husband, and her daughter came to my foster home. The lady was so kind, with a smile that lit up her eyes when she saw me. She asked why I was being sold. My foster mother said that it was because I wouldn't amount to much, and she couldn't show me. I didn't understand what she meant, because she kept showing me to different people a lot. Then she stated she only showed quality dogs. Wow, now that was another blow to my bruised ego. The new lady picked me up, and told my foster mother that her daughter sent her a picture of my on-line photo, and they came to check me out. It was love at first sight.

When my new Mommy got me home, she taught me how to do a high five, and tap my forehead for the I love you sign. That was our special sign. I show Mommy every day how much I love her. Sometimes I give the high five signs to people that show special attention to me. Other times, I do that cute standing up on my hind legs, and waving my front paws routine, and sometimes even talk to her. It gets me special treats.

Life was wonderful, and Mommy, took me everywhere she went. She took me for long walks. She introduced me to our neighbors. She talked to me about everything, because she said I listened, and would not repeat what she told me. We spent a lot of time together in those first few months after I was adopted.

Less than a year later my life changed. My human daddy went to heaven. I never left my Mommy's side, and tried to cheer her up because I knew she was sad. Mommy and

I moved into a new home, and we started to spend more time together because Mommy said I made her happy. I tried to be good, and did all my cute little tricks for her.

Not long afterwards my Uncle Mike, (his real name is Robert Michael, but the family calls him Mike) who lived far away in Georgia got really sick. He was told he needed surgery, and wanted Mommy to come down. I heard Mommy telling Sissy that Uncle Mike would be in the hospital for a long time. For the first time Mommy left me with Sissy for "a short while" she said. After hearing Mommy tell Sissy she would be gone for a while, I wanted to make sure Mommy would never forget me, so I started to write to her every day.

I'm hoping that this book encourages children to be themselves, search out their strengths. It's their unique individuality that will make them shine. Zora was initially led to believe she was destined for greatness. She was, but not as a show dog. Her personality and cuteness stand out, and she captures the heart of all who have the privilege of meeting her. She makes sure she captures the attention of any one she comes in contact with.

This is me being cute. They just love it when I move my front paws up and down, begging for treats.

CHAPTER 1

MOMMY IN GEORGIA

For the first time in my life my Mommy left me for more than a few days, and I wasn't happy. I loved being with my Sissy (that's Mommy's human daughter, Julianne). Sissy lives with her husband, my Uncle Bill, two daughters, Natasha, who doesn't like dogs, but loves cats, and Michala who loves dogs.

They have a dog, who happens to be my best friend, Roxy, and two cats, Jingles, who is always clawing and hissing at me. Nala could be my fur twin, because we have the same color fur. Actually, I have hair and she has fur. Also, she's a cat. Nala is very sneaky, and hides in the girls' bedrooms. After a while it didn't matter that we were all different, we learned to get along, and liked each other despite our differences.

Even though Mommy made sure I was well taken care of, she wasn't there. I wanted to make sure she wouldn't forget me. The people in the other homes I lived in forgot me. I love my Mommy, and even though she sometimes under-stands what I'm barking about, I didn't think that would work long distance. Writing was the only way I could think of to stay in touch.

Hi Mommy!

I want you to know I miss you, and Sissy is taking good care of me. We are all praying for Uncle Mike. I had a nice walk today and ended up sitting in Sissy's lap. Sissy's lap is nice and warm. Yours is better, but don't tell her I said that. Roxy ate all my dinner and the cat's dinner too. I was sad. Sissy fed me ham and more food. Then Roxy vomited. Serves her right! Sissy is going to lock her up when we eat. High five! Wuff you!

Hi Mommy!

I'm eating dinner in the living room so they can make sure I eat. They locked up Roxy so she wouldn't eat my food. Jingles liked my food better, and I liked his so we decided to eat each other's. Uncle Bill was getting mad, and kept trying to get me and Jingles to eat our own food. He has no sense of humor.

Sissy's neck is really bothering her, and she has a headache. She told me the next time I bark she's going to put me in the microwave. l think she's kidding because l barked again and she didn't. I'm playing with Roxy and having fun.

Everyone is going to Michala's concert tonight, so we have the house to ourselves. Give Uncle Mike a big lick from me.

High five! Wuff you!

Good Morning Mommy!

See the blanket I'm lying on? Natasha gave it to me because l jumped on it. She said "Ewe, this disgusting thing jumped on my blanket she can have it." Sissy yelled at her for that and told her to be nice to me. I'm just glad l got the blanket. It's so soft. Sissy and Uncle Bill rolled up the rug in the living room. You poop one time on the rug last year and they never let you live it down. Geez!

I've been a very good girl and have been playing nice with everyone. Michala has been very nice to me, but Natasha doesn't like any dogs so she is mean to me and Roxy. I think I'm going to make a mess on her blanket before l leave. We're all still praying for Uncle Mike.

High Five! Wuff you!

Hello Zora.

Thank you for your informative messages. I'm glad Sissy, Uncle Bill and Michala are nice to you, and that you are finally getting along with Jingles. Give Jingles a lick from me and tell him you'll be nice to him from now on.

Your cousin Larry said that if Natasha continues to be mean to you, you have his permission to make a mess on her blanket. Thank you for not doing the same on Sissy's rug because you may need to stay with her again.

Please give everyone kisses from us and tell them we love them and are grateful for all of your prayers for Uncle Mike. High Five, Wuff you too.

Mommy

Oh Mommy,

I forgot to tell you something else funny. Natasha favors the cats and Nala pee'd in her clean clothes hamper. I thought it was funny. Sissy was not happy neither was Natasha. Sissy is busy and I'm being a good girl. I'm so sick of all of you making pierogi all the time. I hope I get to go for a nice walk today. It's beautiful outside. High five! Wuff you too!

Hello Mommy!

See that sweet little smile on my face? I'm being a good girl. Sissy says it's a mischievous smile because she blames me for peeing on the floor. There are three other animals living here so she can't prove its mine. I didn't act guilty.

I'm glad to hear Uncle Mike is out of surgery. Give him high five from me. I miss you, but l am having lots of fun. Natasha took me for a walk yesterday.

Today is a yucky rainy day. (You know l don't like going out in the rain. Don't tell Sissy then she'll know it was me who pee'd on the floor). Sissy is doing a happy dance because she's about to finish the last of the cheese pierogi. I get to spend the weekend playing with the girls, I'm so excited! High five. Wuff you!

(Mommy was supposed to come home, but I heard her telling Sissy she needed to stay a little longer. Uncle Mike wasn't better, and she wanted to make sure "he was out of the woods". I didn't know he was in the woods, I thought Mommy told me he was having an operation in the hospital. Grownups, I wish they would say what they mean.)

Hi Zora.

Please be a good girl for Sissy, Uncle Bill, Natasha, and Michala. I need them to take care of you a couple more days. Be extra nice to Jingles and Nala. Also, don't bug Roxy so much, otherwise Sissy may lock you up. No more peeing on the floor, that's not allowed. It will be our secret as I don't want Sissy to get mad at you. Make sure you keep smiling sweetly that way they will feel guilty for scolding you. Just continue to be your sweet self. Please give everyone a lick from me. Hugs, Kisses, High Five I love you.

Mommy.

Hello Mommy!

I'm sitting in Sissy's lap. I had such a good time last night. Michala and Uncle Bill took Roxy and l for a long walk. I had so much fun smelling all the new scents. Roxy rolled around and got all muddy and had to get a bath. Sissy fed me chicken and it was so good.

Roxy keeps playing with my squeaky toy. We're having so much fun. We play all the time. This morning l had some scrambled eggs for breakfast. Sissy wouldn't give me a lot because she said my breath finally smells normal and she won't give me a lot of people food. She said you spoil me. I miss you and all the yummy treats you give.

Nice Reddi Whip picture that Uncle Larry sent, by the way. The Apple Fritters looked yummy. Tell Uncle Larry to behave and give Uncle Mike kisses from me.

High five. Wuff you!

Evil Max

CHAPTER 2

THE EVIL MAX

Sissy's brother, my Uncle Ted stopped by with his son, my cousin Colin, and their new pet, a dog. They called him Max, we nicknamed him the evil one. Mommy hadn't met him yet. I couldn't wait to write Mommy about him.

Mommy!

Save me! See that thing in the photo? His name is Max and he's evil. He belongs to Colin, who is hiding behind the couch. Wonder why? Max keeps biting me and Roxy, and we're running away from him. He may be little but he's scary! I'm hiding on Sissy's lap. Roxy is playing with MY squeaky toy. I can't wait till this evil little thing leaves. Oh, and did l mention he's so scary!

High Five! Wuff you!

Mommy!

That evil dog is on my blanket and playing with my squeaky toy! Roxy and l don't like him. He keeps biting us. I can't wait till they leave. The only good thing is, Natasha thought Max was so cute and took him to her bed and he peed in her bed! Sissy is annoyed because l won't leave her lap. Miss you! High Five! Wuff you!

Mommy!!!! ❤

I'm so excited!!! Sissy told me Uncle Mike is doing better and you're coming home tomorrow. I'm so happy! Everyone is nice here but our home is a lot quieter. There are always people coming and going here. All the animals! I DO NOT like that Max. Wait till you meet him. I can hide in your lap. Evil little dog! They should have named him Diablo or Satan. I'm so excited to go home.

High five! Wuff you!

Zora,

My little angel, Mommy misses you too. Tomorrow, after I pick you up, when we get home I'll give you a special treat for being such a good girl. It's hard to be at someone's house. You think the family is getting on your nerves, but hard as it is to believe, you may be getting on theirs.

Just remember Mommy loves you and will see you soon. I sent you some pictures of Mommy, and your soon to be new family and friends. You will just love them, Sherry and Bruce. Sherry is retired RN and Bruce heads up horse shows. Maybe he'll let you chase some horses someday. Hugs and Wuff you back.

Mommy

CHAPTER 3
HOME, AND THEN GONE

Mommy came home for a few weeks, and I was so excited to have her home. I couldn't keep my paws off of her. Everywhere that Mommy went, I made sure she took me, that is when she could. Would you believe there are still some places that dogs aren't allowed?

Dear Uncle Larry, my new Aunt Sherry, Uncle Bruce and my new fur cousins Justin and Wesley.

I don't know where to begin to thank you for taking care of my Mommy. She is very special to me, so it's good to have her back. Don't get me wrong Sissy, Uncle Bill and the girls were gracious hosts, but Sissy squealed on me to my Mommy. She told her I pee'd twice in the house, but I really never do that at home. Honest, cross my little heart. It's just that it was raining and Mommy takes me for a walk with an umbrella. Sissy was shoving me out the door, and that's just not right. I hate wet hair. Anyway, I really am good. Mommy said she may take me for a ride to Georgia.

I've never been in Georgia. So, if I come I don't want you to worry. I will only pee and do that other nasty stuff outside. I'm really enjoying Mommy's lap right now. Doggie hugs and kisses to all of You, especially Uncle Mike. Wuff you all.

Mommy was home for a few days, but then my cousin Larry called and told Mommy that Uncle Mike was not doing better, and had a setback. He asked if Mommy could come back to Georgia. Uncle Mike was not responding as well as the doctors thought he should. Larry told Mommy that they really needed her. So, once again I was staying with Sissy, but now I knew the rules of their house.

Good Morning Mommy,

I'm still tired and trying to rest. This house is so busy compared to ours. Even Sissy said she wanted to sleep in but she had to drive Michala to school. I was tired yesterday too.

Roxy is being nice and we're having fun. I haven't even seen Nala, she's been hiding. Jingles and l are getting along better. I was laying by him and he was being nice. He did get annoyed and growled and hissed at me, all because l sniffed his behind. l don't see what the big deal was. Hope everyone is doing better. I'm going to take a nap. Talk to you later. High Five! Wuff you!

Hi Cousin Zora,

What kind of older cousin are you? By the way, this is your cousin, Wesley, Wes for short. I'm nine months old.

Why didn't you warn me that chewing up Uncle Mike's feather pillow would land me in jail? Who knew dead bird feathers could still fly around all over the house? Well not all over, only the living room, dining room, kitchen, hallway, and Uncle Mike's office. What a mess those bird feathers made, and I'm the one getting locked up?

Anyway, back to me. You would think they would give me a chew toy or something when they left. I'm teething, and the pillow was just lying there on Uncle Mike's bed, calling to me.

Oh, and you haven't met your other cousin Justin yet. He's tougher than me, and the king of this castle. Did anyone even think to blame him? No. They wouldn't dare. I look forward to meeting you some day.

So how does Jingles smell? Did you get punished for sniffing him? I bet not. Can you come bail me out? HELP. Ruff, Ruff.

Wesley

Hi Mommy,

I hope you received that picture of Michala I sent you. She started softball today and had two games. She's a catcher, and looks good suited up. They lost the first game but won the second. Michala got a double and made it to home plate twice. Sissy was good and came home between games to let us out. Good thing she did.

Roxy got a bath yesterday and smells good. We both got to eat liverwurst.

Yummy. Sissy is about to clean up house. After the games she came home and made spinach and artichoke dip. She's complaining because she can't sleep at night. Nothing else really new here. I hope Uncle Larry is calmer with you there, and Uncle Mike is doing better. I got a note from Wes, is he going to be okay? High Five! Wuff you!

Dear Cousin Zora,

Tell our Aunt Sissy that your Mommy said to give her a big hug and to tell her thank you for taking such good care of you. Your Mommy showed us Michala's baseball picture and told us how proud she was of Michala. Wow, a double play. Good for her. Can't wait to meet all of you including the other fur cousins, Roxy, Nala and Jingles. Not sure the fur cats will be safe around us.

By the way we watched your Mommy making meat-balls with Italian sausage and beef. They were yummy. She gave Justin and me one. You lose out. Found out your Mommy knows how to rough it. Not much in the way of cooking utensils left here, no colander, and she managed to cook spaghetti.

Then your cousin Larry and Mommy took everything to the hospital to eat lunch with Uncle Mike. They left the hospital around 3:30 in the afternoon to come home early to fix a salad for Uncle Mike. Early didn't work out. The valet people lost your Uncle Larry's car. After waiting for over 1 1/2 hours Larry had to go help them find the car. Ha-ha gave us more time to have the run of the house.

By the way, this is Wesley, they finally let me out of jail.

Write you more later little cousin. Hugs to all the human's and fur cousins.

Ruff Ruff from Wesley and Justin

Happy Mother's Day Mommy!!!

I had yummy chicken! So good I'm licking my lips. Sissy is annoyed she's not having a good Mother's Day. She's drinking vodka and tea now, and can't wait till after dinner to have the chocolate covered strawberries that she made.

Michala is still cleaning her room since last weekend. It's taking her forever. You can get lost in her bedroom. Natasha is self-absorbed. Natasha is about to make Fettuccini Alfredo for dinner. Sissy has leftover chicken from yesterday and spinach, so it will be a good meal. Her friend Julie is coming over because Sissy feels bad she's all alone. Bri is here because her mom left town. I miss you.

High Five! Wuff you!

Mommy!

I hope Uncle Mike is better. Also, I hope cousin Larry is a little less stressed.

I can't wait to sit in your lap.

High Five! Wuff you!

Hi my little conniving fur baby, Zora,

I know that you were licking your lips so that Sissy will give you more chicken. Leave Sissy alone, after all it's her Mother's Day too.

Uncle Mike got an early reprieve and he is home from the hospital for a while. It looks like if he has to go back, it will only be for a very short visit.

Wesley told me to let you know he had jail time again. He didn't realize that chewing the corner of his expen-

sive bed was not allowed either. He is sad because not only did he get jailed but scolded big time by Larry.

Justin wanted you to know he's still top dog, and is behaving. Justin hops down the stairs like a rabbit. It is both funny and cute.

Well, we are all going to sit down to beef stroganoff over boiled potatoes, which I prepared by popular request. Unfortunately, the potato masher moved to Florida with the other utensils.

Well, my little one, be good, and Mommy will buy you your favorite treat when I get home. Love you, gives lots of kisses and hugs to all my girls and Uncle Bill too, of course.

Mommy

Dear Zora,

Mommy is sorry she hasn't written sooner. I'm glad Sissy is taking good care of you. I was hoping Natasha got to like you, but oh well, it's her loss. Mommy misses you a lot, especially at night. Please continue to be a good girl, and at least I know Michala, Sissy, Uncle Bill and the other fur babies are good to you. I *still have a cold, and am doing everything I can to get over it. I made Schnitzel today for dinner, and apple fritters for breakfast. Uncle Mike and Bruce enjoyed the apple fritters. We will be eating dinner soon.*

Love to all, and a high five.

Hi Mommy!!!

I'm sleeping on the couch in Roxy's usual spot. I took it over! I was so tired, that my tongue fell out of my mouth. Sissy said I was snoring, but you know I don't snore.

I got everyone here trained well. I won't even eat my dog food till Sissy puts real food in there. I've been very good. I was so excited to hear you're coming back a day earlier. I'm glad to hear Uncle Mike is home from the hospital too. Next time you go there l want to go too so l can meet Wesley and Justin. We would have so much fun. Sissy is making a ham today so l can wait to eat my dinner.

High Five! Wuff you! ❤

Can you tell the girls aren't happy? Natasha was upset
with me and picked up Nala to get her away from me.
Michala picked me up for the same reason.

CHAPTER 4
MOMMY IS ON THE ROAD, AGAIN

Mommy was invited to a birthday cruise for her cousin Eva's daughter, Sandy. They live in Florida. I don't like water that much, so I stayed home. Which meant I was going to stay with Sissy, Uncle Bill, and my cousins. Yippee. Mommy's new friend Lee was driving Mommy down, so I knew she'd be safe on the road because she had company for the trip.

Hi Mommy!!!

I'm having so much fun. The girls aren't happy with me because l keep bulling Nala all the time. I showed her who's boss.

Sissy keeps lifting me up in her chair so l can sit on her lap. Don't tell her your lap is better. Hope you and Lee are having a good time. I sure am.

Miss you. High Five! Wuff you!

Dear Zora,

We are so happy to hear that Nala is getting a break from your antagonism, but how many times must I tell you that you are a guest, and must behave. You really do have to learn how to get along better. Find a common interest.

Also, don't butter up to me that you like my lap better than Sissy's.

On another note Mommy found out that all the hotels are not what they advertise. Mommy and Lee are roughing it today. Oh well, have to check out things better before any future trips.

Tomorrow we will see Noah's Ark, and then leave Kentucky for a new adventure, and hopefully a better hotel.

Behave yourself, and thank Sissy, Uncle Bill, the girls, and your fur cousins for taking care of you. High 5, Wuff you more. Mommy and Lee.

Dear Zora,

What a hectic day! We checked out of the hotel this morning, grabbed a quick cup of coffee, and then went to the Ark. The Ark is HUGE. We took lots of pictures to show you when we get back.

There were only replicas of animals on the Ark. We found out there was a variety of dinosaurs. We learned so many interesting facts about the Ark. There were many species of animals, much more than I had initially thought.

The real animals that are kept on the premises are housed in the Zoo. Not as many as we thought would be there. We didn't go visit the live animals, as we didn't have that much time. Also, we were tired after four hours of walking, and have to leave in about an hour to get back on the road. We did buy some great fudge at one of the shops.

Did you happen to notice that lady that snuck into our Ark photos that we sent? She snuck in not once but twice. Hmm she was just nosy.

Lee and I liked the garden area best. They had bushes shaped into the different animals, including elephants, giraffes, dinosaurs, and even an ostrich.

We are now in Calhoun, Georgia for the night. We ate dinner at Ruby Tuesdays in Tennessee, and thought of Natasha, who claims she wants to move to Tennessee after she graduates. Whew, we are beat. Miss you. Wuff you. Give a big high five to everybody. Love you.

Mommy and Lee

Hi Mommy!!!

I had fun today. Aunt Cheryl came over for dinner. Sissy and her took Roxy and l for a nice walk. Roxy and l played nice today and relaxed on the couch together. I still keep going after Nala because it's fun.

I miss you and Lee. This house is a lot crazier than ours.

High Five! Wuff you!

Dear Zora,

Mommy and Lee have been busy. We are spending time Uncle Mike and Larry, and met some of their friends. Your cousins Wesley and Justin keep barking at us, and still can't get used to us, though Justin sits by Lee when he can. Larry explained that Lee was sitting in Justin's usual spot, that's why he was staying by Lee, but I think it's because he likes Lee. Wesley seemed to favor me after he calmed down.

We met Larry's Sister Debbie (Cricket) and her husband Doc. They have a big farm, and have chickens, and lots of Chihuahuas. Chihuahuas are small dogs that I believe come from Mexico.

I got to see and hold blue eating eggs from Americans chickens. I was told that they are real eggs to. I took pictures of the eggs, and will show you when we get home. It's been raining quite a lot. We miss you and everybody back home. Love, hugs and kisses.

Mommy and Lee

Hi Mommy!!!

Sissy is so selfish. She made herself yummy fried eggs this morning. Well l think they were yummy. She wouldn't share. Jingles and l stared at her and begged and licked our lips because they smelled so good and NOTHING! I know YOU would have shared. I even begged so cute with my little front paws waving and, making my whirring sound though my throat. That didn't work. Oh well. She's been sharing dinner with me though, and taking me for nice walks.

Yesterday Sissy's friends Karen and Julie walked us. It was fun. Especially when Sissy's pants started to fall down and she was holding a leash, and trying to pick up the presents Roxy and l left for her. She couldn't lift the pants back up. Her friend Julie did it for her.

Well I'm going to play. Hope you're having fun! Tell everyone l said hello and high five! Wuff you! Miss you and, your eggs that you would have shared.

Mommy!!!

I'm so glad you are almost home. I'm glad you are off that boat. We've all been so worried about you. Everybody kept talking about the big hurricane Irma that's heading toward Florida. They say it's going to be a really big one.

I've been such a good girl. There's been a lot of rain and scary thunder and lightning. l have to share Sissy's lap with Roxy. Her recliner is too small for both of us. Sissy gets crabby because she feels like she's wearing a fur coat.

I'll see you soon and l can't wait to go home.

High Five! Wuff you!

Dear Zora,

Our adventure is still not over. We had a flat tire taking an alternate route in Florida due to the heavy volume of traffic evacuating trying to outrun the hurricane. Lee swerved to avoid hitting a boy on a bike. Triple A was supposed to be here by now, but we are still waiting.

Oh well, I always did enjoy adventure. It's more fun when there's company. A few people offered to help, but we let them know Triple A was on their way. Hmmm, should have let them help. It may be a bit longer before we can pick you up.

Love you. Hugs to all. Mommy and Lee

Hi Mommy and Lee!

Blurry pic but it took Sissy like 10 tries because l kept moving and licking my lips. Dinner was delicious. I had pork and gravy mixed into my food because l wouldn't eat.

I got Sissy wrapped around my finger. I also went for two nice walks. Sissy gave me my blanket, it's so soft. Having fun.

High Five! Wuff you!

My adventure at Sissy's was over for a while. Mommy and Lee came home safe and sound, and a lot later than they thought they would. Fortunately, Hurricane Irma did not catch up to Mommy. We did get a lot of rain after Mommy and Lee came home.

We had so much fun after we got home. Lee takes really good care of me, and I found out he really likes me, though I don't think he's too happy with my bad breath. I heard him telling Mommy. Mommy does give me milk bone treats, and dental sticks, but I guess it's not helping much. Oh well, she tries. I don't see what the big deal is because I can't smell my breath. Mommy did try to brush my teeth, that wasn't happening. Dental sticks, and mouth wash will have to do. Mommy ended up taking me to my veterinarian doctor.

CHAPTER 5

FLORIDA BOUND

Mommy and Lee decided to take a break from the winter weather. They took a trip to Florida with my Aunt Mary and Uncle Paul. Once more I was taken over to Sissy's and Uncle Bills home. At least now I get along with all my fur cousins, and I'm growing on my human cousins. I'm looking forward to getting spoiled, and waiting for my letters from Mommy.

Good Morning Zora dear.

We woke up to frosty weather in Wytheville Virginia, where we stopped for the night. 39 degrees and cold. It was so cold Lee went to the car to get some long pants. Lee finally listened to Mommy about wearing long pants.

We are so glad Sissy is taking such good care of you. We do miss you at the foot of our bed, keeping our feet warm. Please tell Sissy, Uncle Bill and your cousins we send our love. Tell Sissy I will call her when we get to Savannah, unless she needs to talk sooner. If she does, please ask her to call. I didn't make the call because I didn't want to wake anybody up at the early hours we get up. Love, hugs and high five.

Mommy and Lee

Good Morning Zora,

Today we are going on a historical Trolley ride throughout Savannah. I found out the South is extremely dog friendly. Everywhere we go there are people with dogs which makes us miss you more. There aren't too many people with cats. There are quite a few dog friendly hotels.

On another note downtown Savannah is really beautiful. I will try to send photos of all the historical and pretty places. We took a stroll on the River Walk. Had a nice dinner at one of the restaurants, and there were people outside sitting at tables with their dogs.

The tour guide took us to areas where one of my favorite movies, Gone With the Wind, was filmed.

Tell Sissy, Uncle Bill and my girls, I miss them very much. Please try to get along with your fur cousins, and have fun. Hugs, love you, high five.

Mommy and Lee

Hi Mommy and Lee!

I'm sleeping on the top part of the couch. I've been a good girl. I miss you a lot, and I was sad yesterday.

I slept with Uncle Bill in the big bed for most of the night. Sissy's right, he snores but 1 thought of you. Not because of the snoring. I miss you but I'm having such fun so don't worry. High Five! Wuff you!

Hi Zora.

We just finished touring Savannah, which by the way is BIG on ghost tours, though we didn't take one. Lee and I couldn't get Aunt Mary and Uncle Paul interested in the Ghost tour. Though after we got back to the hotel room they said they wouldn't mind taking a ghost tour the next time we visit Savannah.

The city is beautiful, and there is so much history here. We would love to come back for a week at least.

They are big into the arts here. Also, a lot of historical buildings from the 1700's and 1800's. We are going back to the hotel for an hour, then back to the city for dinner. Miss all of you. Please give everyone Hugs and smooches. Love you, stay sweet, and high five.

Mommy and Lee

Hi Mommy and Lee.

I'm sleeping on my new blankie, the pink one I showed you, and I'm having so much fun with my new toy that l took from Roxy.

I'm out of breath from squeaking and chewing the past 15 minutes. I'm being good but Sissy called me a brat for growling and biting at Roxy. It was her fault for trying to take my toy. Sissy is petting Roxy now but who cares, l got the toy.

High five and wuff you all!!!

Zora,

You must learn to share with Roxy, particularly since it's her new toy. I'm glad Sissy is being so nice to you in spite of you acting like a spoiled brat. A pink blanket, a nice toy, you better make sure you show your appreciation.

We're leaving in the morning to see Uncle Mike, Larry, Bruce, Wesley and Justin. Now those two male fur cousins would have chewed you up and spit you out if you had taken their toy. Be a good girl. Hugs, high five, love you

Mommy and Lee

Mommy,

It's MY toy. I love it. ⬜ I'm still playing with it.

Wesley and Justin don't scare me. Hugs to everyone. I have to keep playing because Sissy said she's taking the annoying toy away from me soon.

High Five! Wuff you!

Hi Mommy and Lee! ❤

Having so much fun here. I've been a good girl. Roxy and 1 played yesterday and had fun. It snowed again. Sissy and 1 wish we were with you. Well 1 better get back to napping in front of the warm fireplace. Wuff you and high five!

Good Morning Zora,

Haven't heard from you for a while so I'm guessing you are having way too much fun. Uncle Paul is not feeling well today, maybe a cold, or a sinus infection. Lots of pollen in the air. Hope he feels better because we are going to a comedy talent show tonight. Hope everyone there is doing fine, and that you are playing nice with Roxy, Jingles and Nala. Say hi to everyone from us, hugs and kisses, high five.

Mommy and Lee

Hi Mommy and Lee!

Busy day here today. Sissy had to drive girls to school and she's been paying bills and running to the bank. She's all excited because Friday she is getting a new dishwasher and cooktop. She also called someone about delivering pierogi, but is waiting to hear back.

I've been playing nice with everyone, except Nala. She's a big baby and runs away from me. I even licked her once to show her l was friendly and she hissed at me and tried to claw me. Jingles is ok. Roxy and l play sometimes. Sissy is the best. Her lap is nice like yours. Hope you are all behaving and having fun. I miss you.

High Five! Wuff you!

Hi Mommy and Lee!

I'm having a nice relaxing day sitting on Sissy's lap. I just ate dinner. I get golden mushroom soup added to my food and it's so good. I miss you but I'm spoiled here. I can sit wherever l want.

Michala had me and Nala playing today. Nala always runs away from me but Michala held her up by me and l got to lick her. Ok. I'm going to take a nap now. Hope you all are having fun. Miss you and high five.

Hi Mommy and Lee!

Four more days and l get to see you! I've had fun here but l can't wait to get home. Too many other little creatures here. I like when it's all about me.

Sissy is being very good to me. I'm tired so I'll talk to you later. Hope you're having fun.

Wuff you and high five!

Hurry home Mommy and Lee!

I don't want to tattle on Sissy, but she's very stingy with the treats. There's so many animals here that l have to share time with them. I like it when everyone only has me to give their attention too. Also, nobody here appreciates what a good watch dog l am.

Wuff you! High Five!

Good Morning Mommy and Lee!

I slept on the couch with Roxy and Michala. I had sweet dreams about seeing you, and Lee, and sleeping in our bed tonight.

I had fun here but sure do miss you both a lot. Michala said she'll miss me.

I've been such a good girl. I went potty outside all the time, even in the rain. Sissy didn't use an umbrella either. I even started to play with the cats a little. I kissed Jingles and stopped bullying Nala. Drive safe. See you soon.

High five! Wuff you! ❤

Dear Zora,

I love the picture of Michala, with you and Roxy. Lee and I miss you bunches, and can't wait to see you, hopefully by six o'clock this evening. I'm glad you are playing nice with all the fur babies. Make sure you thank Sissy and Uncle Bill by giving them lots of extra licks. The weather here in West Virginia is chilly but sunny.

Hugs and kisses, and high five, from Lee and Mommy to all.

All is well. Mommy and Lee made it home safe and sound. They also promised me that they will not leave me behind anymore, but will take me with them when they travel. I told them I didn't mind staying with Sissy and the family, but I'm glad they missed me as much as I missed them. Now when we travel, I can write letters to all my family, and let them know what we're doing. I can't wait for my new adventures.

High Five Zora Print